D1716434

Bullying

Questions
and Feelings
About...

PICTURE WINDOW BOOKS
a capstone imprint

by Louise Spilsbury
illustrated by Ximena Jeria

Questions and Feelings About . . . is published by
Picture Window Books, a Capstone imprint
1710 Roe Crest Drive, North Mankato, MN 56003
www.mycapstone.com

U.S. edition copyright © 2020 by Picture Window Books, a Capstone Imprint

Library of Congress Cataloging-in-Publication Data is available on
the Library of Congress website.

ISBN: 978-1-5158-4541-6 (library binding)

Editor: Melanie Palmer
Design: Lisa Peacock
Author: Louise Spilsbury

First published in Great Britain in 2018
by The Watts Publishing Group
Copyright © The Watts Publishing Group, 2018
All rights reserved.

Printed and bound in China.
001593

Most people get along well most of the time. They are kind to each other and treat each other fairly.

Why is it important to be kind?

Some people are not kind. They do and say things to make other people feel sad, scared, embarrassed, or angry. This is bullying.

Bullies usually say or do mean things to hurt or upset people on purpose. They behave unkindly, often more than once.

It is not bullying if a friend is rude when you argue or if someone hurts you by mistake and they say sorry afterwards.

Some bullies tease people or call them bad names. They say mean things about a person to hurt their feelings.

Bullies who use words to mock or taunt
sometimes say they are only joking.
But bullying is never, ever funny.

*How does it feel to be called
a bad name?*

Some bullies push, pinch, kick, or hit people. They might do this to hurt or scare someone whenever they get the chance.

Bullies may also take someone's belongings. They may threaten to hurt that person if they don't do what the bully wants.

Some bullies try to persuade or bully other people to gang up on one person. A bully might try to leave a person out of games, parties, or outings.

How do you think it feels to be left out of a game or group?

Bullies may also send nasty messages using a mobile phone or computer. A bully may post information, photos, or videos about a person online to hurt or embarrass them. This is called cyberbullying.

It is particularly bad because bullies can send horrible messages at any time to reach people anywhere.

When someone is bullied it can make them feel very lonely. They can feel as if no one likes them, even though that's not true.

They might stop sleeping, eating properly, doing school work, and having fun.
They might even feel so sad that they get sick.

If you are bullied, the most important thing to do is tell an adult. There are many people who will listen and help.

You could tell a parent, a relative, or a teacher. If you find it hard to talk about, you could write it in a letter.

Who do you talk to when you need help with a problem?

It's not a good idea to fight back if someone hits you. Try not to call a bully names if they insult you. The bully could get nastier and you could get into trouble, too.

Just tell an adult
about the bullying.
Adults can make
the bullying stop.

21

Bullying is a problem that can happen to anyone.
If someone is bullied, it is never their fault.

A bully might pick on something a person does or says or the way they look. That is just an excuse. A bully just wants to be a bully.

There is no excuse for bullying, and it is always wrong. But did you know that bullies often have problems? Knowing this can make bullies seem less powerful or less scary.

Some bullies have problems at home or have been bullied themselves.

Bullies often hurt others to try to make themselves feel bigger or better.

Bullying is bad for everyone, even the bully.
But bullies can change. They can stop being
unkind and unfair.

Bullies can get help to sort out their problems.
They can learn to be kind. They can say sorry.

How do you feel after saying sorry for doing something wrong?

What would you say or do to cheer someone up?

We can all help to stop bullying. We can not join in or laugh with a bully, or we can ask an adult to stop the bully. Be kind and friendly to anyone who has been bullied so they do not feel alone.

We should all treat other people as we would like to be treated and think about other people's feelings. That way we will all feel happy and cared for!

Notes for Caregivers

This book can be a useful way for families and professionals to start a discussion with children about bullying. Bullying can have a serious and damaging effect on children in the short and long term, so it's vital to help children talk about bullying.

Young people who are bullied may not always tell adults, as they may be afraid or ashamed. It's important to help children understand what bullying is, what different forms it can take, and what can be done to stop it. Children can be confused about bullying and think falling out with a friend is bullying. Help them understand that when someone says or does something intentionally hurtful and they keep doing it—even when you tell them to stop or show them that you're upset—it is bullying.

Being open and discussing bullying can help children deal with it. Knowing that adults take bullying seriously and will listen to a child's problems makes it more likely that children will report bullying. Talking about bullying calmly and sensibly also shows a child that's the best way to take action. It helps children understand that while a child being bullied needs support and bullies need to be stopped, a child who bullies others can also be helped and learn to make better choices in the future. Talking about bullying is a chance to discuss empathy. It teaches children how to treat other people fairly and kindly and to think about how their actions impact others.

Group Activities

1. Talk about how people should treat each other with respect. Have each child make their own set of rules about behaving fairly and kindly.

2. In order to encourage children to celebrate differences, choose pairs of children who don't usually play or sit together. Each pair should ask each other questions (Examples: What games or foods do you like? What do you do really well? What do you like best in a friend?) The pairs should write down at least three answers and present them to another pair of students.

3. Ask children to create an anti-bullying poster to raise awareness of the issue in school.

4. Ask children to write a story about a bullying incident and how it was resolved. The children (or an adult) could read the stories out loud and ask the children to discuss how the stories make them feel.

Read More:

Bracken, Beth. *The Little Bully* (Little Boost). Picture Window Books, 2012.

Dewdney, Anna. *Llama Llama and the Bully Goat*. Viking Books for Young Readers, 2013.

O'Neill, Alexis. *The Recess Queen*. Scholastic Press, 2002.

Read the entire Questions and Feelings About . . . series:

Adoption
Autism
Bullying
Having a Disability
Racism
When Parents Separate
When Someone Dies
Worries